# *A Bushwhacker's View of the Adirondacks*

# *A Bushwhacker's View of the Adirondacks*

John E. Winkler

North Country Books, Inc.
Utica, New York

A Bushwhacker's View of the Adirondacks



ISBN 0-925168-37-8

Library of Congress Cataloging-in-Publication Data

Winkler, John E., 1941 -
A bushwhacker's view of the Adirondacks / by John E. Winkler :
[edited by Neal Burdick]. — 1st ed.
p. cm.
ISBN 0-925168-37-8
1. Hiking—New York (State)—Adirondack Mountains--Pictorial works.
2. Hiking—New York (State)—Adirodack Mountains—Guidebooks.
3. Adirondack Mountains (N.Y.)—Pictorial works. 4. Adirondack
Mountains (N.Y.)—Guidebooks. I. Burdick, Neal S. II. Title.
GV199.42.N652A3498 1994
796.5'097475—dc20 94-44156
CIP

Printed in Hong Kong

First Printing 1995

*Cover photo:* Crane Mountain from Moose Mountain. USGS ***STONY CREEK*** quad - 1968
*Photo page ii*: Autumn at Lily Pad Pond.

Published by
North Country Books, Inc.
18 Irving Place
Utica, New York 13501

Dedicated to my mother,
Margaret I. Winkler

PAINTED TRILLIUMS

# *Contents*

A VIEW OF MT. HAYSTACK FROM THE WEST PEAK OF GOTHICS

# *Acknowledgments*

This book would have been difficult to assemble without the help of several people. I would like to thank Kathleen Gill, Jim Goodwin, James Papero (DEC at Raybrook), Diana Strnisa, Bruce Wadsworth, Bill White and the staff of the Adirondack Research Center for their contributions.

Special thanks, also, to my many friends who accompanied me on numerous bushwhack excursions: Eugene Brousseau (who introduced me to bushwhacking), Scott Ebeling, John Francini, Kathleen Gill (who has accompanied me on more bushwhacks than anyone), Kiernan Ryan, Peter Shafran, Frank Sorbero, Stephen Sopko, Thomas Stanwood, Diana Strnisa, John Wiley and Michael Vinci.

Also to be thanked is my mother. Whenever I leave for a hike, which is usually 4:30 a.m., she always gets up and prepares my breakfast. Even though she need not do this, I have truly appreciated it.

The pen and ink sketches and cartoon were drawn by John Wiley, who was an active member of the Schenectady Chapter ADK for twelve years. He is well remembered for designing the Chapter's current patch. John is also a member of the Adirondack 46ers. He currently resides in Lynnwood, Washington with his wife, Elise Kessler Wiley, and is a member of the *Mountaineers* hiking club in the state of Washington.

The three "ramblings" in this book were written by a former neighbor and friend, Carl W. Uschman. Handicapped with multiple sclerosis, he greatly enjoyed drives into the Adirondacks, which inspired him to write. Mr. Uschman lived all of his life in Schenectady. He worked for the General Electric Company and also the former ALCO Products, before retiring on a disability pension in 1947; he died in 1971.

Editor Neal Burdick is a native of the North Country and a graduate of St. Lawrence University, where he is publications editor. He is a free-lance writer and the editor of the Adirondack Mountain Club's magazine, *Adirondac*, as well as its eight-volume series of guides to trails in the Adirondacks and Catskills. He lives with his family in Canton, New York.

# *Introduction*

Many books have been published about the Adirondacks, from its early history to the present, about special events and people, guide books, even Adirondack songs and folklore. Several excellent photographers have published album-type books depicting Adirondack scenes.

This book is different! Most of the pictures were taken in places where few people hike, let alone photograph: the remote trailless areas. Many of these places required long hours of intense bushwhacking to reach, while others were only a short distance from a trail.

This book is not intended to encourage, promote, or be used as a guide book for bushwhacking. One who is inclined to do so should be thoroughly familiar with map and compass reading, and use the latest maps available. Many lands in the Adirondacks are private, and occasionally easements change. Some lands which were previously open to the public are now posted.

The majority of the photos in this book were taken in the High Peaks Region of the Adirondacks, near Lake Placid and Keene Valley, in Essex County west of Exit 30, I-87 (the Adirondack Northway). Most of the highest mountains in the state are located in this area.

Quite often more than one mountain, stream, pond or lake will bear the same name. To help identify the location in which the pictures were taken, a map reference is given by each photo or group of photos. The maps quoted are the USGS 7.5 x 15 minute metric series of 1978-79 and 1989-90, unless otherwise noted.

According to the USGS surveys of 1953/54 and 1978/79, forty-two mountains are over 4,000 feet (two of which are 5,000-plus footers). In 1872, an Albany resident, Verplank Colvin, convinced the New York State Legislature to hire him to make the first accurate survey of the Adirondacks. Colvin contributed much to the Adirondack history in many ways through his writings and lobbying the legislature—he was the leading advocate for the formation of the Adirondack Park.

In 1898-1902, the first United States Geological Survey was done in the Adirondacks, and forty-six peaks were determined to be 4,000 feet or more in height. The first USGS topographic maps of the area were then produced.

In 1948, an organization called the Adirondack 46ers was founded and anyone who climbs the original Adirondack 46 mountains can join. As of December 31, 1993, 3,371 persons reported climbing the forty-six. In the same year, a record number of climbers was reported for a single calendar year—184, according to Grace Hudowalski, the club historian.

After I became a 46er in 1975 (#1279), I decided to bushwhack all of those peaks not using any trail or herd path. A herd path is an unmaintained trail that has developed from the herds of people ascending the peak via the same route.

Today, some 285 miles of foot, ski and horse trails exist in the High Peaks Region. Only one or, at most, two sides of the major mountains are trailless. These, then, would have to provide my bushwhack routes.

I soon discovered there was a good reason why there were no trails or herd paths on these sides of the mountains; they were the most difficult sides to ascend. So bushwhacking the forty-six was quite a challenge!

Getting companions to go with me was somewhat of a problem also, as most hikers do not like to bushwhack rough terrain. I did some of the peaks solo, but did have friends accompany me on most.

It took ten years to bushwhack all of the forty-six mountains. As far as I know, I am the only person in modern times to do so. The Adirondack Forty-Sixers awarded me the number "B-1" in addition to my regular number.

After completing this project, I continued to bushwhack into remote ponds and lesser-known mountains that were trailless. I did most of this within the High Peaks Region.

# *Historical Facts*

The Adirondack Park was created in 1892, and is the largest of its kind in the contiguous forty-eight states. Comprised of 9,375 square miles or about six million acres, it is approximately the size of the state of Vermont, or two and a half times as large as Yellowstone National Park in Wyoming. Permanent local residents number about 130,000 (as of 1991). The Park is within a one-day drive for seventy million people, one quarter of the population of the United States! Some 10 millions people enter and use the park each year.

In the late nineteenth century, extensive logging was done in the High Peaks as well as other areas of the Adirondacks. The enormous amount of slash that was left behind set the stage for a devastating fire in June 1903, which burned 465,000 acres of forest. Also consumed in that fire was the original Adirondak Loj (at Heart Lake). It was one of the largest log structures in the world at that time. Built by Henry Van Hovenberg, it took two years to complete, opening in 1880. The years 1908 and 1913 saw two more devastating fires in the Adirondacks.

In September of 1929, then Governor Franklin D. Roosevelt turned the first spade of earth, and construction was started for the building of the Whiteface Memorial Highway. Six years later, President Franklin D. Roosevelt dedicated the opening of the new highway. The total cost of the project was $1,250,000.

In the 1930s and 1940s automobiles would often overheat during the six-mile long climb, but today's autos are much more advanced and this is no longer a problem.

Lake Placid is the only place in North America to have hosted two Winter Olympics —1932 and 1980. For the 1980 Olympics, new bobsled and luge runs, ice arena and ski jumps were constructed, and roads in the region were improved.

In 1972 the state legislature created the Adirondack Park Agency, which regulates land use and development in the park.

On November 25, 1950 (the Saturday of Thanksgiving weekend), winds around 100 mph blew down about a half million acres of timber in the High Peaks. This storm ended Noah John Rondeau's hermitage that he had along the Cold River for nearly fifty years. He was one of the more notable hermits who lived in the Adirondacks.

June 1963 saw yet another of nature's effects on the mountains. A six-inch rainfall on Giant Mountain sent tons of rocks, trees and dirt down the mountain's west side, creating many of the rock slides that are, today, popular climbs.

Stillwater Inlet, Marcy Swamp.

USGS ***MOUNT MARCY*** quad - 1976

## *ADIRONDACK WILD*

These mighty mountains, verdant forests,
  rushing streams and quiescent ponds,
Varied little by seasonal changes,
Is our inheritance,
A great gift endowed for our solace,
A tonic for the soul.
It is our obligation among the grandeur
  of God's workshop,
To appreciate, respect, enjoy and learn,
Not to despoil.
To develop an awareness,
  a genuine appreciation for it all.

C.W. Uschman

*Previous Page:* Late autumn woods near Lindsay Brook

USGS ***WITHERBEE*** quad - 1978

Chapter One

# *Mountain Vistas*

A High Peak View from Peaked Hill, in the Pharaoh Lake Wilderness Area

In Chapter One are viewed a lot of the familiar peaks, but from unfamiliar places. Some photos were taken while bushwhacking the forty-six peaks, while others were shot from lesser-known trailless areas and mountains.

Many of these familiar peaks originally had names which today are unfamiliar to most of us.

Algonquin Peak was known as Mount McIntyre. Today, Wright, Algonquin, Boundary, Iroquois and Marshall mountains are known as the McIntyre Range.

Iroquois was first known as Mount Clinton, and that name was later changed to what is now known as Marshall. USGS maps of the area show Marshall as Clinton as late as the 1953 series.

Mount Colden was originally known as Mount McMartin, after Duncan McMartin, an early developer of the McIntyre Iron Works that was near Tahawus.

"Ragged Mountain" in the Seward Range is known today as Seymour Mountain.

A 1909 New York State Forest, Fish & Game Commission map has Mount Colvin labeled as Mount Sabael.

Mount Henderson is now known as MacNaughton Mountain. Today, Henderson Mountain is a 3,752-foot peak just east of Bradley Pond.

Hunter's Pass (between Mount Dix and Nippletop) was once known as "Gorge of the Dial."

Popular Heart Lake was known early as Clear Lake.

Winter wonderland on Pitchoff Mountain (3,600').

USGS ***KEENE VALLEY*** quad - 1979

On this very steep bushwhack of Mount Colvin from the Lower Ausable Lake, one of my two companions wonders if we can conquer this one. We did!

USGS ***MOUNT MARCY*** quad -1979

## *NORTH RIVER MOUNTAINS*

The next three photographs were taken from a desolate and trailless range in the southern High Peaks Region southeast of Tahawus, known as the North River Mountains. The highest peak in this range is Rist Mountain (3,860') and it is fifty-sixth on the list of the 100 highest Adirondack peaks. The one-mile-long ridge took over twelve hours to bushwhack from start to finish. It has the thickest woods ever traversed to date.

USGS ***SANTANONI PEAK / MOUNT MARCY*** quads - 1979

Boreas Ponds from Rist Mountain.

Santanoni and Panther Peaks from Rist Mountain.

Mount Marcy, The "Great Range," Giant Mountain, Nippletop and Dix Mountain, from Rist Mountain.

View of Rocky Peak and Giant Mountain from an open area between Oak Hill and Iron Mountain.

USGS ***ELIZABETHTOWN*** quad - 1979

Sawtooth Mountains from Mount Seymour.

USGS ***AMPERSAND LAKE*** quad - 1978

Looking up at a rocky ledge on Algonquin Peak's northwest side.

USGS ***KEENE VALLEY*** quad - 1979

# SHEPHERD'S TOOTH

Only a quarter mile down from Iroquois Peak's southwest side is a rock out-cropping called "The Shepherd's Tooth." Many hikers traversing the McIntyre Range, overlook this nice little "peak." From Iroquois it is only a fifteen minute trek down to it. A canister, uniquely placed on its summit, contains a log book to record your name. A portion of the write-up found in the register is as follows: "The first persons known to admit to climbing Shepherd's Tooth were some young members of the Schaefer and Zahniser families, led by (the late) Carolyn Schaefer who crossed it in 1956 in another vain attempt at reaching the summit of Mount Marshall. They named the peak, but for some other reason never returned. This temporary register was placed here by the Buffalo Boys . . ."

If one chooses to bushwhack from the "tooth" down to the Lake Colden / Indian Pass crossover trail, note that it will be steep and the woods will be quite dense.

Prior to her death in 1985, Carolyn Schaefer owned and operated "Skyline Outfitters" in Keene.

USGS ***AMPERSAND LAKE / KEENE VALLEY*** quads - 1979

Iroquois Peak from "The Shepherd's Tooth" (4,400').

Negotiating a cliff on the east side of Santanoni Peak.

USGS ***SANTANONI PEAK*** quad - 1979

## *WALLFACE MOUNTAIN*

Wallface Mountain, so named for its 1,000-foot-high rock face, is a trailless peak of 3,700 feet. Number seventy-one on the Adirondack 100 highest list, it is located five miles southwest of Adirondac Loj, adjacent to Indian Pass. While the summit is wooded and has no views, excellent views are found on the northeast end of the mountain near the top of the headwall. As late as July and early August, snow and ice can be found in the caves near the top of Indian Pass.

USGS ***AMPERSAND LAKE*** quad - 1979

From the west side of Mount Marshall is a good view of Wallface Mountain.

Mount Marshall from Wallface Mountain.

McIntyre Range from Wallface Mountain.

Moose Pond and MacNaughton Mountain from Three Peaks (2,950').

USGS ***AMPERSAND LAKE*** quad - 1978

East side of Whiteface Mountain.

USGS ***LAKE PLACID*** quad - 1979

Elk Lake and the High Peaks from Clear Pond Mountain (2,977').

USGS ***MOUNT MARCY*** quad - 1979

View looking south from Peaked Hills.

USGS ***BLUE RIDGE*** quad - 1979

Checking the compass on a bushwhack up the northwest side of Cliff Mountain. Iroquois Mountain and "The Shepherd's Tooth" are in the background.

USGS ***MOUNT MARCY*** quad - 1979

## *PANTHER GORGE: AN UNFORGETTABLE EXPERIENCE*

This is one of the most wild and beautiful places in the Adirondacks. It is located between Mount Marcy and Mount Haystack, in the heart of the High Peaks. Ebeneezer Emmons named Marcy in honor of Governor William Marcy who inaugurated the first geological survey of the state. Orson Phelps, a 19th century guide in the Adirondacks, named Mount Haystack as its summit rocks resembled a stack of hay.

In the summer of 1979 I spent a week of my vacation backpacking in the Adirondacks. One of my goals was to spend a couple days exploring Panther Gorge. I arrived there late one afternoon, and made camp at the entrance to the gorge. I spent the remainder of the day exploring the area. After supper I hung my food (mostly the freeze-dried variety) high up between two trees to be safe from the animals. My backpack was hung on a tree branch about six feet from the ground. Since it contained no food I thought this was good enough.

All was quiet until about two a.m. when I was awakened by a clawing sound nearby. I looked out of my tent and in the bright moonlight spotted a rather large bear clawing at my pack. I banged on my Sierra cup to make noise which soon sent the bear back into the woods. I then went over to see what damage was done and discovered it was after something in the side pocket of the pack. In that pocket was a can of foot powder. His sharp claw punctured not only the thin pack cover, but also the metal can! I removed the can, cleaned the sweet smelling powder off the pack and then buried the now leaky can of powder under a large rock. During the remainder of the night, I heard bears walking about, but they didn't bother me or anything else of my belongings.

The next morning when I got up, I noticed the rock and the can of foot powder had been dug up. Apparently the sweet-smelling powder attracted the bear, or he had a foot problem! I spent this day exploring and taking pictures of the gorge. It was a beautiful, sunny and clear day.

My second and last night, with the foot powder can empty, was quiet and peaceful.

Today, beavers have made dams in the gorge, and that has changed its appearance slightly. Panther Gorge is one place I'll never forget.

USGS ***MOUNT MARCY*** quad - 1979

Mount Haystack from Panther Gorge.

Marcy Brook, Panther Gorge.

Headwall, Panther Gorge.

Avalanche Lake, Avalanche Mountain (3,800'), Lake Colden and the Flowed Lands, from Calamity Mountain (3,620').

USGS ***SANTANONI PEAK / MOUNT MARCY*** quads - 1979

Armstrong Mountain, from Gooseberry Mountain (approximately 3,850').

USGS ***KEENE VALLEY*** quad - 1979

## *BEAUTIFUL WOODS — OPEN SUMMITS*

One of the nicest areas in the High Peaks Region for bushwhacking is the area west of I-87 between exits 29 and 30, and east of paralleling Route 9. There are many little mountains here between 2,000 and 3,000 feet with open summits and fine views. The next five photographs were taken in this general area.

Camel's Hump and Niagara Mountain, because of their excellent views, are two of the most popular bushwhacks in this region.

On Old Far Mountain, the remains of a small private airplane which crashed in the early 1980s killing its lone occupant (a clergyman) can be found.

This area is also very popular with hunters and fishermen.

USGS ***WITHERBEE*** quad - 1978

Macomb Mountain, from Camel's Hump (2,720').

Mount Dix from Howard Mountain (1,710').

View from Old Far Mountain with East Dix in the background.

Moriah Pond from Broughton Ledges.

Blue Ridge (3,440') from Wyman Hill (2,224').

USGS ***BLUE RIDGE*** quad - 1979

Panther Mountain (3,865') from an unnamed peak (3,170') about two miles northeast of Cedar River Flow.

USGS ***INDIAN LAKE*** quad - 1990

Mount Dix from the east side of Nippletop.

USGS ***MOUNT MARCY*** quad - 1979

Saddleback Mountain from Point Balk (approximately 4,200').

USGS ***MOUNT MARCY*** quad - 1979

The Great Range as viewed from Point Balk.

Mount Haystack as seen from trailless Little Marcy (4,765').

USGS ***MOUNT MARCY*** quad - 1979

Woods on the east side of the Blue Ridge.

USGS ***BLUE RIDGE*** quad - 1989

## *LOST POND PEAK*

Approximately four miles southwest of Adirondac Loj is Lost Pond Peak. At 3,900' it is forty-seventh on the Adirondack 100 highest list. This completely trailless mountain has one of the best views, in my opinion, of any non-46er peaks. If it were a 46er peak, I'm certain its view rating would be in the top ten. The panorama of the McIntyre Range is magnificent. The ponds are well hidden among the lesser summits of the mountain, and therefore cannot be seen from any other mountain.

USGS ***AMPERSAND LAKE*** quad - 1978

Seward Range from Lost Pond Peak.

Algonquin, Boundary and Iroquois Peaks from Lost Pond Peak.

A view from Huckleberry Mountain (2,010').

USGS ***HOPE FALLS*** quad - 1990

Crane Mountain (approximately 3,220') from Moose Mountain (2,831').

USGS ***STONY CREEK*** quad - 1968

Calamity Mountain from an abandoned beaver pond along Calamity Brook.

USGS ***SANTANONI PEAK*** quad - 1979

Chapter Two

# *Lakes and Ponds*

LAKE MARIE LOUISE AND ROCKY PEAK RIDGE

Many of the some 2,800 lakes and ponds in the Adirondacks are next to trails, or have trails leading to them. Numerous others are hidden between the mountains and have no trail access. Some of these are pictured in this chapter.

Today beavers live in a lot of these ponds and have even created some of them.

In the late 1800s, lumber companies constructed many dams to assist in logging operations. During the 1930s, the Civilian Conservation Corps rebuilt many of these dams.

Marcy Dam, which was originally built by the J. J. Rogers Company of Ausable Forks around the turn of the twentieth century, was one of the first to be rebuilt (1933). But the dam lacked in design to prevent plunge pool action—the creation of a hole and circular current so close to the dam as to undermine it. During 1964-66 the DEC rebuilt the dam with chutes that led the falling water away from the dam. The plunge pool is now some yards farther downstream.

In the 1850s, the McIntyre Iron Company built a dam on the Flowed Lands to send more water down Calamity Brook to operate a smelter, the remains of which are still standing below the Upper Works trailhead. In the early part of the twentieth century the dam was rebuilt to enable pulp logs to be floated down Calamity Brook on their way to Finch, Pruyn Paper Mills in Glens Falls. The gorge of Hanging Spear Falls would have made log driving difficult via the Opalescent River.

The spring floods of 1979 severely damaged the dam, and in 1981, the DEC fully breached the dam for safety reasons. The Flowed Lands once again became a marshy area as it was originally. The bridge and dam will not be rebuilt.

Howard Zahniser once declared that the Flowed Lands was one of the most beautiful lakes in the Adirondacks, the equal of Jenny Lake in the Grand Tetons. Zahniser was president of the Wilderness Society from 1946 to 1964. He was also the major lobbyist in persuading the U.S. Congress to pass the National Wilderness Act of 1964. He died shortly before the bill was passed and signed by President Lyndon Johnson. The act set aside a number of forest areas in the United States, such as the Bob Marshall Wilderness Area of Montana, as areas where man is a visitor who does not remain.

Bogs, swamps and marshes also are plentiful in the Adirondacks, covering about 900,000 acres or fifteen percent of the wildland area.

All but four photos in this chapter were taken in the High Peaks Region.

The bridge and dam on the Flowed Lands as it looked in the early 1970s.

USGS ***MOUNT MARCY*** quad - 1979

Flowed Lands and the McIntyre Range from the bridge, early 1970s.

Black Pond, between Three Peaks and the Sawtooth Range.

USGS ***AMPERSAND LAKE*** quad - 1978

Dial Mountain and Dial Pond.

USGS ***MOUNT MARCY*** quad - 1979

Moss Pond.

USGS ***MOUNT MARCY*** quad - 1979

Mount Marcy and Moss Pond.

Mount Allen from an unnamed pond near Cheney Cobble.

USGS ***MOUNT MARCY*** quad - 1979

Round Pond, east of Sharp Ridge Campsite.

USGS ***WITHERBEE*** quad - 1978

Rhododendron Pond.

USGS ***WITHERBEE*** quad - 1979

Algonquin Peak and Wright Peak from Lower Wallface Ponds.

USGS ***AMPERSAND LAKE*** QUAD - 1978

Lost Pond and Lost Pond Peak.

USGS ***AMPERSAND LAKE*** quad - 1978

This small pond in Caribou Pass lies between Avalanche Mountain (3,800') and Algonquin Peak.

USGS ***KEENE VALLEY*** quad - 1979

Mount Colden from Henderson Lake.

USGS ***SANTANONI PEAK*** quad - 1979

Unnamed pond west of Wyman Hill.

USGS ***BLUE RIDGE*** quad - 1989

A remote beaver pond approximately 5½ miles north-northeast of Rand Mountain.

USGS ***HOPE FALLS*** quad - 1990

Middle Lake.

USGS ***HOPE FALLS*** quad - 1990

Murphy Vly.

USGS ***HOPE FALLS*** quad - 1990

Murphy Vly.

Chapter Three

# *Streams and Waterfalls*

CASCADES ON THE BOQUET RIVER, NORTH FORK

Streams and waterfalls are in abundance throughout the Adirondacks and the Northeast. One does not have to bushwhack to find them. However, except for two, all of the photos in Chapter Three were taken in trailless areas of the High Peaks Region.

O.K. Slip Falls, which descends into the Hudson River Gorge below Blue Ridge, is visible to rafters running the Indian and Hudson Rivers to the town of North River. Having a sheer drop of almost 200 feet, this waterfall is credited with having the highest single drop in the Adirondacks.

T-Lake Falls (USGS *PISECO LAKE* quad - 1990), a series of cascades dropping about 350 feet, is also credited as one of the Adirondacks' highest falls.

Roaring Brook on Giant Mountain in Keene Valley has a drop of 290 feet, however, it isn't a continuous drop. The upper part of 180 feet drops into a pool below, where there is another 110-foot drop. From a distance, the two drops appear as one.

Hanging Spear Falls, located a half mile south of Flowed Lands, is another high waterfall in the Adirondacks. William Redfield estimated it as having a drop of around 80 feet. There is also a series of several smaller falls above the main 80-foot drop.

### *MIGHTY 'LIL CREEK*

Flowin' lazily through the woodlands,
Streaked with silver and covered by sunset gold,
I have my moods;
Now serene, now tempestuous.
But I'm goin' places,
For I have a rendezvous with the sea.
Most things on this earth
have a short span of existence;
But I go on and on forever.

C.W. Uschman

Unnamed stream and falls between Street Mountain and Lost Pond Peak.

USGS ***AMPERSAND LAKE*** quad - 1978

Upper West Mill Brook, east side of Macomb Mountain.

USGS ***MOUNT MARCY / WITHERBEE*** quads - 1978, 1979

Unnamed stream south of West Street Mountain (4,034').

USGS ***AMPERSAND LAKE*** quad - 1990

A tributary of Gill Brook on the northwest side of Dial Mountain.

USGS ***MOUNT MARCY*** quad - 1979

Unnamed stream and waterfall on the south side of Mount Marshall between Indian Pass and Calamity Brook.

USGS ***SANTANONI PEAK*** quad - 1979

Mountain Ash along an unnamed stream on the south side of Mount Marshall.

Blowdown on an unnamed stream on the south side of Mount Marshall.

A scenic stream on Mount Marshall's south side.

Roaring Brook southwest of Street Mountain.

USGS ***AMPERSAND LAKE*** quad - 1990

Unnamed stream on the east side of Santanoni Peak.

USGS ***SANTANONI PEAK*** quad - 1979

Fairy Ladder Falls.

USGS ***MOUNT MARCY*** quad - 1979

South Fork Bouquet River, near Mount Hough.

USGS ***MOUNT MARCY*** quad - 1979

View from Uphill Brook.

USGS ***MOUNT MARCY*** quad - 1979

Ausable River.

USGS ***KEENE VALLEY*** quad - 1979

Huge ice chunks on East Stony Creek, spring 1983.

USGS ***HOPE FALLS*** quad - 1990

Frink Brook, Middle Grove State Park.

USGS ***MIDDLE GROVE*** quad - 1967

Chapter Four

# Rock Slides . . .

A SLIDE BUSHWHACK UP THE EAST FACE OF DIX MOUNTAIN

In the High Peaks Region there are hundreds of rock scars or slides on the mountains. A few are pictured here in Chapter Four.

In the last few years (1991-1993) several new slides have occurred on the north side of Mount Dix, and one on the east side of Mount Colden.

Most slides occur when heavy rains fall during the spring thaw, or during a localized heavy summer thunderstorm, on the steep slopes where the soil cover is thin over the massive underlying rock base, and water run-off is concentrated into a narrow stream bed. Earthquakes are relatively minor (thus far) in this part of the country, but they too could create landslides or rock slides.

Many slides have today become popular climbing routes, such as those on Giant, Dix's west side, Colden's east side, Macomb, East Dix, Nippletop, Wright Peak and Whiteface. Others may be too steep, too remote, or not as accessible, and therefore are less often climbed.

The massive slides on the northwest side of Mount Colden, geologists claim, separated a once rather large lake into what is now two lakes—Colden and Avalanche. The debris from the slides was so vast that Avalanche Lake has an elevation of 2,863'—nearly 100 feet higher than 2,764' Lake Colden!

Mount Colden from the east side of Algonquin Peak.

USGS ***KEENE VALLEY*** quad - 1979

View from a slide on Mount Dix's north side.

USGS ***MOUNT MARCY*** quad - 1979

## *PYRAMID PEAK ROCK SLIDES*

Anyone who has climbed Sawteeth Mountain on a clear day has viewed, from the summit, the slides on a pyramid-shaped peak just south of Gothics Mountain. At approximately 4,600' it is popularly called "Pyramid Peak." I think these are the most awesome and dramatic of any slides in the area. The next three photographs were taken from these slides.

USGS ***MOUNT MARCY/ KEENE VALLEY*** quads - 1979

Upper Ausable Lake from the Pyramid slides.

Mount Dix from the Pyramid Peak rock slide.

Looking up at the Pyramid Peak rock slides.

Top of the “Bottle Slide” on Giant Mountain.

USGS ***ELIZABETHTOWN*** quad - 1978

View of Gothics while climbing a rock slide on the south side of Saddleback Mountain.

USGS ***MOUNT MARCY / KEENE VALLEY*** quads - 1979

Rock slide on the east side of Mount Colden.
USGS ***MOUNT MARCY / KEENE VALLEY*** quads - 1979

Moose Pond from the west side rock slide on Santanoni Peak.
USGS ***SANTANONI PEAK*** quad - 1979

From the summit of Mount Dix, this photograph of the East Dix Mountain rock slides was shot on infrared film. As well as showing "false colors" it also accentuates the rocky areas.

USGS ***MOUNT MARCY*** quad - 1979

Rock slides on Mount Macomb as seen from Elk Lake.

USGS ***MOUNT MARCY*** quad - 1979

A rock slide on the east side of Giant Mountain in winter.

USGS ***ELIZABETHTOWN*** quad - 1978

View from the top of the Beckhorn rock slide.

USGS ***MOUNT MARCY*** quad - 1979

The Wright Peak rock slide as seen from the east side of Algonquin Peak.

USGS ***KEENE VALLEY*** quad - 1979

Nippletop rock slide.

USGS ***MOUNT MARCY*** QUAD - 1979

## *MOUNT MARSHALL'S ROCK SLIDES*

On a challenging bushwhack of Mount Marhsall's south side, via an unnamed stream which flows into Calamity Brook, two impressive rock slides were encountered. Near the stream's beginning, the westernmost slide, which has a grade of twenty degrees, makes for an easy ascent. It is an old slide with excellent views of Mount Adams and the North River Mountains. From here, the bushwhack over to the summit of Mount Marhsall is horrendous to say the least! This slide is visible from the summit of Mount Adams.

On a second bushwhack in this area, the easternmost slide was climbed. This is a newer slide which appears to have been formed in the late 1970s or early 1980s. This slide has a much steeper grade—thirty degrees. From this one, excellent views of the Santanoni Range, Henderson Lake and the last unnamed summit in the McIntyre Range can be seen. This slide is visible form Santanoni Peak and also from the Calamity Brook trail in late fall through early spring when the leaves are off of the trees, .02 miles east of the suspension bridge that crosses Calamity Brook.

USGS ***SANTANONI PEAK*** quad - 1979

Rock slides on Mount Marshall's south side.

Mountain Ash berries and the McIntyre Range from the easternmost rock slide on Mount Marhsall's south side.

Mount Adams (3,540') as seen from the westernmost rock slide on Mount Marshall's south side.

USGS ***SANTANONI PEAK*** quad - 1979

North River Range as seen from a rock slide on Santanoni Peak's east side.

USGS ***SANTANONI PEAK*** quad - 1979

Chapter Five

# *Woods Sculptures and Flora*

AN ADIRONDACK FOREST IN THE HIGH PEAKS

The Adirondacks, and especially the High Peaks Region, have an abundance of "woods sculptures," both on and off the trail. The strange and unique rock formations (like that of Chimney Mountain), the many twisted root systems, and the numerous designs which can be imagined amid an area of blowdown, are unique "sculptures" of the Adirondacks.

Wildflowers can be seen everywhere. The flora pictured in this chapter are some of those which are less frequently seen, or their names are not as well known as other more common species. The Goldenrod photo is the lone exception.

While most of these flowers can be found throughout much of the eastern half of the United States and southeastern Canada, the blooming times stated are for the Adirondack region. Flowering times in other areas may be earlier or later.

Some of the photos in this last chapter were taken on bushwhacks, while others were photographed near trails in various regions of the Adirondacks.

A cross country skier stops to admire the "candy cane" snow formation atop this old tree stump. Photographed near Preston Ponds.

This unusual pink cloud formation over Noonmark Mountain was photographed from the Ausable Club in Keene Valley, on a cold January day at sunset.

A rock engulfed by a tree. Photographed southwest of Stephens Pond in the Blue Ridge Wilderness area.

Photographed at the north end of Elk Lake, a winter storm is approaching from the southwest..

Chimney Mountain.

USGS ***THIRTEENTH LAKE*** qaud - 1990

Sunset, central Adirondacks.

Although it appears to be in bud, the flower of the CLOSED or BOTTLE GENTIAN (Gentian family) can be found in moist meadows during August and early September. Photographed at Elk Pass.

INDIAN PIPE (Indian Pipe family). This saprophytic plant with an average height of five inches can be found during the mid-summer months growing in areas of rich humus in the woodlands. Photographed near Hunters Pass.

FRINGED POLYGALA (GAYWINGS) (Milkwort family). This petite little flower can be found in moist woods in May-June. Photographed near Stephens Brook west of Bald Peak.

ROSE POGONIA (Orchid family). This rare flower blooms in late June and early July in wet meadows, swamps and bogs. Photographed at Lens Lake.

SHOWY LADYSLIPPER (Orchid family). This seldom-seen variety of ladyslipper grows in swamps and moist woods, blooming in June and early July. Photographed along Black Creek.

USGS ***OHIO*** quad - 1989

NORTHERN PITCHER PLANT (Pitcher Plant family). This carnivorous plant is found in sphagnum bogs blooms in July and August. Photographed in a bog on the south side of Mount Marshall.

Leaves of the NORTHERN PITCHER PLANT in late autumn.

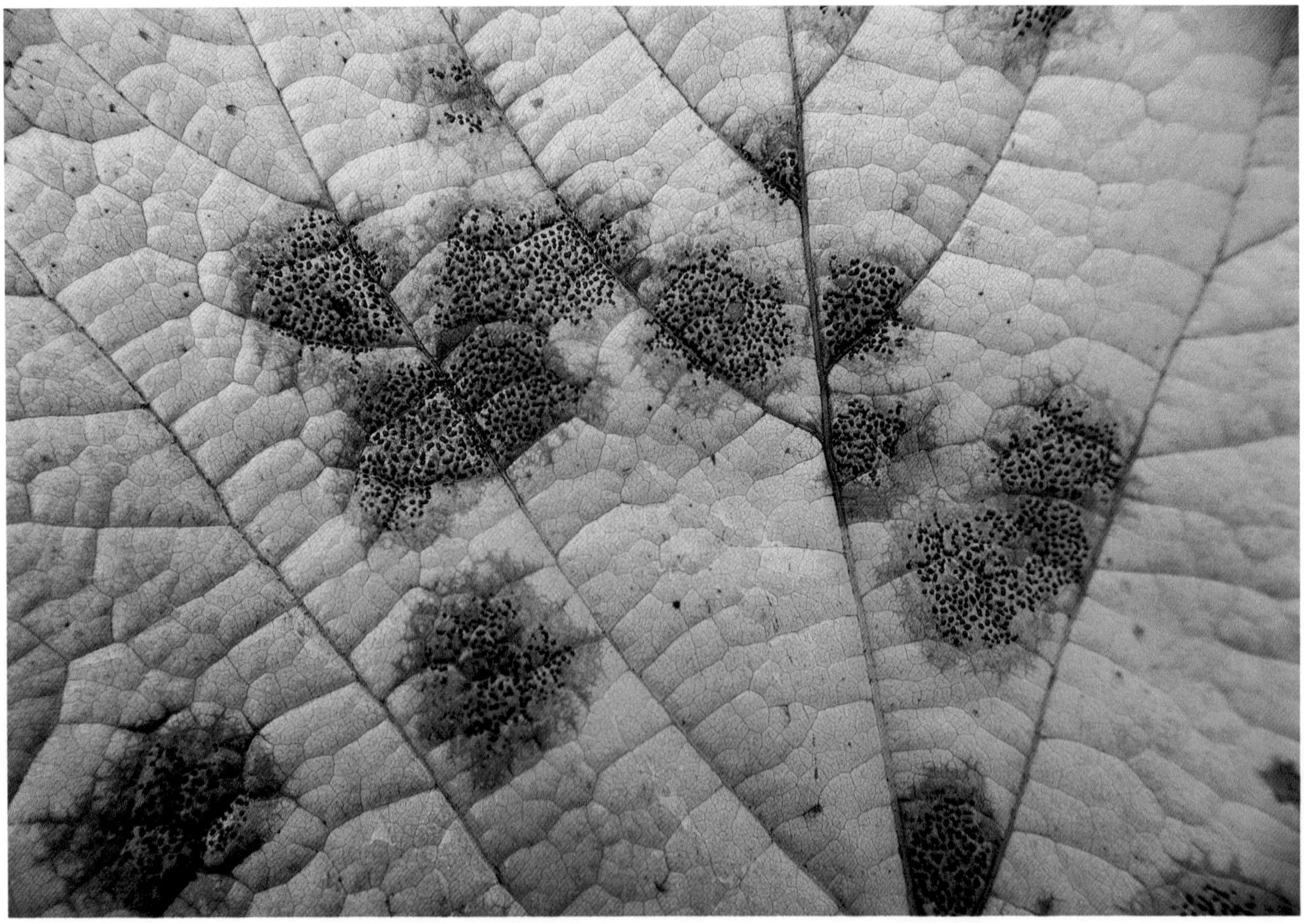

Leaf mold on a STRIPED MAPLE leaf. This rather small tree with a height of only fifteen to twenty feet and large leaves is common in the Adirondacks.

MOUNTAIN SANDWORT (Pink family). These delicate Alpine-type flowers bloom during the summer months in rock crevices above the timberline in the Sub-Alpine zone (4,500-4,900 feet), and the Alpine Zone (4,900 feet and above). Although these plants have adapted to grow in a harsh environment, they have no defense against hikers' boots!

The yellowish-green chinky lichen on the rocks in the background is MAP LICHEN. It is commonly found throughout the Adirondacks as well as North America. Photographed on Mount Haystack.

## *FAIR, THE LONE MOUNTAIN FLOWER*

Here, above timberline on an Adirondack summit,
Where the air is clean and pure, is this diminutive flower.
Destined to grace a desolate place.

To bloom in all its glory,
So the high climbing adventurer can sense its beauty.

The killing frosts soon call a halt to its energetic growth.
Recalled by Nature to the dormant state,
under a blanket of protective snow and ice.

Until another season, when the warmth of a new sun,
will once again urge the display of its hardy and
noble character, in these restricted surroundings,
to become a thing of beauty.

Guided to maturity by Nature's blessing touch.

C.W. Uschman

FRAGRANT WATER LILY (Water Lily family). This distinctive blossom can be found in ponds from late June through August. Photographed at Stony Pond.

YELLOW RED POLYGORE are found during the summer mostly on dead conifers, but sometimes on hardwoods as well. Photographed near Cheney Cobble.

LARGE FLOWERED (WHITE) TRILLIUM (Lily familiy). Much more rare than the red and painted trilliums, it blooms in May and June in woods with neutral soils. Photographed near the hikers' register at the Ausable Club.

PAINTED TRILLIUM (Lily family). Generally similar but smaller than the white trillium, these blooms can be found in May and June in moist woodlands with acidic soil. This rare four-leaved, four-petalled specimen was photographed on Three Peaks Mountain.

COMMON SHADBUSH (Rose family). Its name coincides with the New England shad fish which spawns at the same time the bush blooms. With a maximum height of forty to fifty feet, its blooms can be seen in late May and early June. Photographed near Baldhead Mountain.

TALL GOLDENROD (Sunflower family). This common wildflower has some 125 species, most of which grow in eastern North America. It blooms in August and September in fields, clearings and along roadsides.

A VIEW OF THE GOTHICS FROM THE PINNACLE

# *Back Country Tales*

In bushwhacking the 46 highest peaks, I have found Mount Colvin to be the most difficult, with Mount Haystack a close second.

On Colvin I was fortunate to have two good-natured buddies, Michael and Kiernan, go with me. First we backpacked to Elk Pass via the Gill Brook trail, where we set up camp. At one p.m., we took our day packs and climbed Colvin via the trail, continuing down the other side to just above the Lower Ausable Lake. From here we bushwhacked along the State/AMR property line halfway across the base of the mountain, and at four p.m. started the bushwhack back up Colvin. This side of the mountain is extremely steep, and many times we thought we would not be able to make it. But somehow, with a lot of perseverance and determination, we did. It took five hours to reach the summit once again, almost at dark. Very tired, we then headed down to our camp at Elk Pass. After a late dinner, we retired for the night.

Before dawn it started to rain, and continued to do so until later that morning. Getting up at eight a.m. and still tired from the previous day's expedition, packing up all that wet gear in the rain was no fun. However, before we reached the parking lot the sun came out, making a pleasant ending to an unforgettable weekend.

Bushwhacking Mount Haystack was a long, long day and somewhat complicated. We had to hike almost to the top of Sawteeth and then bushwhack down the west side to Shanty Brook, where we made camp. From here we took day packs, bushwhacking over to Haystack Brook and then climbing the east side of Haystack. Through very thick spruce woods and quite steep all the way, this was a long, tough haul. Since we were camped over at Shanty Brook, we had to bushwhack back down the mountain as well. We never arrived back at the campsite until one a.m.! Just my friend Frank and I were on this trip, and we still don't know how we managed to find the tent after bushwhacking in the dark for three and one half hours. The next day we had to bushwhack with the large packs back up Sawteeth, where we would once again pick up the trail and hike out.

In my twenty years of bushwhacking, I've been off course a few times, occasionally confused for awhile as to just where I was, but was never really lost to the point of spending an unexpected night in the woods, or having to be searched for by rangers or rescuers.

In the mid-1970s, and relatively early in my bushwhacking career, three good friends, John, Scott and Tom, and I attempted to bushwhack from Mount Emmons to Mount Seymour in the Seward Range. On a Friday evening, late in August, we hiked in six miles from Corey's to Ward Brook and set up camp. Early Saturday morning we took our day packs and climbed Seward, Donaldson and Emmons via the herd paths. From the summit of Emmons we took a compass bearing for Mount Seymour and started down the mountain into Oulouska Pass. The woods were dense and the going was slow. As we were about to start the ascent of Seymour from the pass, we noted that the time and terrain were not going to allow us to complete this trip as planned. Only moments after checking the compasses and walking a short distance, we discovered a small stream which appeared to us to be flowing north. It was here we decided to abort the bushwhack of Seymour, follow the stream back to Ward Brook and call it a day.

After two hours of bushwhacking, the stream appeared much larger than it should be. John jokingly said, "Wouldn't it be something if we were headed into Cold River instead of Ward Brook!" A quick check of the compasses did indeed confirm that this scenario was true. We were headed south instead of north. A few moments later we met a lone camper who confirmed we were about ten minutes away from Cold River and Noah John Rondeau's old hermitage.

It was dusk when we reached Cold River, and there were only two flashlights for the four of us, which were mediocre at best. Before long, only one flashlight was functional, but we now had a trail system to follow back to camp, which was approximately six miles away.

At Mountain Pond we took a break, resting next to a trail junction sign post. John, Scott and I rested next to the sign, while Tom leaned against the post, which was rotten at the base. It crashed to the ground, nearly knocking John out! It was a long, long day. At one a.m. we finally arrived back at our campsite. Tired, exhausted and too weary to cook supper, we just "crashed" in our tents.

We learned a valuable lesson: Always check the compass. Continuously. One can turn around in the woods very quickly without realizing it.

This reminds me of another incident which is somewhat humorous, but, at the time, was embarrassing. While leading a group of hikers on a Schenectady Chapter (ADK) outing on a bushwhack near Sharp Ridge Campsite up Greenough Mountain, I suddenly began leading the group in circles. Soon we were standing ankle-deep in a bog that I said we were going to avoid! Some time in the mid-afternoon, and for an unknown reason, my compass totally demagnetized. Since I was a competent leader and we were not far from civilization, no one else checked their compasses until we were in this swamp.

Always have others in the party check their compasses and make sure all have the same bearing. Even though most compasses (as mine did) have guarantees against failure, it can happen—although it is rare. The guarantee is worthless in the middle of the wilderness.

# *Be Prepared*

Unprepared hikers can and do have serious problems. Unfortunately, a number of hikers have lost their lives being unprepared for the conditions.

Always carry plenty of non-perishable food such as dried fruits, nuts, candy, carrots, etc., a flashlight with extra batteries and bulb, waterproof matches, space blanket, first aid kit, extra socks, good quality rain gear, map and compass. In May, June and early July, insect repellent is necessary; the black flies can be horrendous this time of year. A long-sleeved shirt, long pants and a head net are also recommended. In cooler weather, wool shirt, polypropylene underwear, extra pants and outerwear for the coolest temperatures anticipated will be necessary. In winter, snowshoes, insulated boots, crampons, ice ax, foam pad, sleeping bag and tarp are appropriate. In spring, snow may be gone in the cities, but still can be quite deep in the mountains, especially in the High Peaks. A good rule to follow is carry snowshoes one hike beyond when you last needed them. In the fall, remember also that snow comes earlier to the mountains than to the low-lying valleys.

Boots are one of the most important items. They should be broken in, comfortable, waterproofed and insulated (in seasons other than summer). Always carry moleskin, should a "hot spot" or blister develop on the foot.

Water is generally found most everywhere in the Adirondacks. However, in recent years it has been recommended to filter the water to guard against giardia, an intestinal parasite. Not all filters will removed this parasite, or viruses. The chemical iodine is an excellent purification method.

Bushwhackers should always be prepared to spend an unexpected night in the woods. Bushwhacking alone is not recommended. Carefully watch the time. This is especially important in seasons other than summer. Turn around at a reasonable hour, even if the objective hasn't been reached.

When backpacking, hiking or bushwhacking, be sure to sign in at the registers located near or at trailheads. Include the length of your stay and destination. Let someone at home or a friend know of your planned route, especially if you're bushwhacking and cannot sign a trail register anywhere. Rescuers have a lot of trouble and waste precious time if they have only a vague idea of where to search in case of a problem.

# *Photographic Notes*

I have two cameras, both Single Lens Reflex (SLRs) with many lenses from 18mm to 300mm, plus a 2X teleconverter. In addition, I use close-up lens attachments in +1, +2, +4 and +10 magnifications. In bushwhacking, a tripod is virtually impossible to set up, although it would be very desirable to be able to do so.

Most of the photos in this book were taken on Kodachrome 64 transparency film. Recently Kodachrome has introduced an ISO 200 rated film which I have found to be very satisfactory and the higher speed is indeed welcome. Now one can use higher shutter speeds in low light areas, lessening the need for a tripod. However, any picture, no matter what the condition, will be better if a tripod can be used.

I also have experimented with color infrared film, one photo of which appears on page 80.

I generally use one of three filters—a polarizer, a pale yellow #81B (reduces bluishness on distant shots as well as giving a warmer tone), or an enhancing filter which is slightly lavender in color and enhances reds, oranges and yellows without having any effect on the other colors. It works especially well in the autumn.

It took twenty years to get enough photos to do this book. With only weekends and holidays in which to go to the mountains, the weather all too often doesn't cooperate. The Adirondacks are not in an area of the country which has an abundance of clear sunny days! Overcast days are unfortunately more the norm. But the mountains have their own special beauty no matter what the weather—even if it doesn't always make for that "great picture."

*Previous Page:* Marcy Brook, near Indian Falls.

# *Clubs and Organizations*

Many organizations are engaged in conserving the Adirondacks. Five are mentioned here.

The oldest Adirondack conservation organization is *The Association For the Protection of the Adirondacks* (AFPA), founded nearly 100 years ago in 1901. Through public education and lobbying activities, it seeks to protect and preserve the forest preserve's "forever wild" status. *The Adirondack Research Center* (ARC), an arm of AFPA, was started in Schenectady by Paul Schaefer in 1979. It contains a large collection of books, magazines, maps, photos, slides, films, paintings and legislative records on the Adirondacks. Much was donated by Schaefer and came from his personal collection.

*The Adirondack Mountain Club* (ADK), headquartered in Lake George, New York, is a nonprofit organization dedicated to conservation, education and recreation in the New York State Forest Preserve. Founded in 1922, ADK has approximately 20,000 members in its twenty-eight regional chapters (as of 1994). ADK's activities include hiking, snowshoeing, white and flat water canoeing, backpacking, winter camping and cross country skiing. The club is active in trail and lean-to maintenance, conducts extensive environmental education workshops and programs, and works on many projects to encourage sound conservation. It is an active, committed group of outdoor-oriented individuals.

*The Adirondack Forty-Sixers*. During the 1970s, use of the Adirondack region exploded. It was at this time the Forty-Sixer organization altered its course. The changing philosophy of the Forty-Sixers was best expressed in 1976 by then president, Ed Ketchledge. He referred to the need for the organization to develop a "stewardship concept." For many years the members had "taken" from the mountains in terms of beautiful views, challenging climbs, educational discoveries and warm memories. But as "Ketch" stated, a debt was owed by all who had "taken" and the Forty-Sixers were going to do their part to repay that debt.

During the early '70s, President Glen Fish offered Forty-Sixer support in the areas of trail maintenance, a litter bag program (48,000 distributed) and a search and rescue unit. In May of 1974, he helped to organize the removal of lean-to garbage pits in the High Peaks area.

The "Forty-Sixer Outdoor Leadership Workshop" was begun in 1972 and continues today. Other projects supported by the organization include summit reseeding, the Trailmaster program, and financial support of various Adirondack Mountain Club projects.

The Forty-Sixers have avoided the larger state-wide issues and have attempted to focus their attention to specific, hands-on solutions to the immediate problems facing the High Peaks. A focus on their public service projects indicates that they have placed their money and time where the greatest positive impact on the High Peaks could be affected. They hope that anyone who takes the time to explore what the Forty-Sixers stand for will agree that they are upholding their stewardship role in the Adirondacks.

*The Adirondack Council*, formed in 1975, is the largest environmental group in New York State. The council represents the Adirondack interests of four member organizations: *The Wilderness Society*, *National Parks and Conservation Association*, *Natural Resources Defense Council* and *Association for the Protection of the Adirondacks*. With a combined membership of over 500,000 (as of 1993), the council's efforts include advocacy and lobbying for Adirondack land use and land protection, as well as research, education, environmental monitoring on the local, state and national levels and litigation when necessary.

Founded in 1971, *The Adirondack Nature Conservancy* (ANC), a chapter of the *Nature Conservancy*, works to preserve plants, animals and natural communities that represent the diversity of life on earth by protecting the lands and waters they need to survive. *The Adirondack Land Trust* (ALT), established to preserve agricultural, forest and open space land resources of northern New York, became its partner in 1988.

ANC/ALT works directly with the people who own the land. Through real estate agreements with landowners, outright purchases and cooperative projects with state and local governments, ANC/ALT already have protected more then 214,000 Adirondack acres. They maintain fourteen preserves totaling 6,604 acres and have transferred 61,405 acres (as of 1994) to the New York State Department of Environmental Conservation.

For more information on any of the above, write:

Association for the Protection of the Adirondacks
(Adirondack Research Center)
30 Roland Place
Schenectady, New York 12304

Adirondack Mountain Club
RR 3, Box 3055
Lake George, New York 12845-9522

The Adirondack Forty-Sixers
279 Rand Hill Road
Morrisonville, New York 12962

The Adirondack Council
PO Box D-2, Church Street
Elizabethtown, New York 12932

The Nature Conservancy
1815 N. Lynn Street
Arlington, Virginia 22209

The Adirondack Nature Conservancy and Land Trust
Box 65
Keene Valley, New York 12943

## *THE MYSTERY PICTURE*

This photo was taken in late August in the High Peaks Region. Can you recognize the view or the site from which it was taken?

# *The Sixty Highest Mountains of the Adirondacks*

| *No.* | *Name* | *Elev.* |
|---|---|---|
| 1. | MOUNT MARCY | 5,344 |
| 2. | ALGONQUIN PEAK | 5,114 |
| 3. | MOUNT HAYSTACK | 4,960 |
| 4. | MOUNT SKYLIGHT | 4,926 |
| 5. | WHITEFACE MOUNTAIN | 4,867 |
| 6. | MOUNT DIX | 4,857 |
| 7. | IROQUOIS PEAK | 4,850 |
| 8. | GRAY PEAK | 4,840 |
| 9. | BASIN MOUNTAIN | 4,827 |
| 10. | GOTHICS MOUNTAIN | 4,736 |
| 11. | MOUNT COLDEN | 4,714 |
| 12. | GIANT MOUNTAIN | 4,627 |
| 13. | NIPPLETOP | 4,620 |
| 14. | SANTANONI PEAK | 4,607 |
| 15. | MOUNT REDFIELD | 4,606 |
| 16. | WRIGHT PEAK | 4,580 |
| 17. | SADDLEBACK MOUNTAIN | 4,515 |
| 18. | PANTHER PEAK | 4,442 |
| 19. | ROCKY PEAK RIDGE | 4,430 |
| 20. | TABLETOP MOUNTAIN | 4,427 |
| 21. | ARMSTRONG MOUNTAIN | 4,410 |
| 22. | MACOMB MOUNTAIN | 4,405 |
| 23. | HOUGH MOUNTAIN | 4,400 |
| 24. | SEWARD MOUNTAIN | 4,361 |
| 25. | MOUNT MARSHALL | 4,360 |
| 26. | ALLEN MOUNTAIN | 4,350 |
| 27. | BIG SLIDE | 4,250 |
| 28. | MOUNT ESTHER | 4,250 |
| 29. | UPPER WOLF JAW | 4,185 |
| 30. | LOWER WOLF JAW | 4,175 |
| 31. | STREET MOUNTAIN | 4,166 |
| 32. | PHELPS MOUNTAIN | 4,161 |
| 33. | DONALDSON MOUNTAIN | 4,140 |
| 34. | MOUNT SEYMOUR | 4,120 |
| 35. | SAWTEETH MOUNTAIN | 4,110 |
| 36. | CASCADE MOUNTAIN | 4,098 |
| 37. | SOUTH DIX MOUNTAIN | 4,060 |
| 38. | PORTER MOUNTAIN | 4,059 |
| 39. | MOUNT COLVIN | 4,057 |
| 40. | MOUNT EMMONS | 4,040 |
| 41. | DIAL MOUNTAIN | 4,020 |
| 42. | EAST DIX MOUNTAIN | 4,012 |
| **43. | MacNAUGHTON MOUNTAIN | 4,000 |
| 44. | GREEN MOUNTAIN | 3,980 |
| *45. | CLIFF MOUNTAIN | 3,970 |
| *46. | BLAKE PEAK | 3,960 |
| †47. | LOST POND PEAK | 3,900 |
| *48. | NYE MOUNTAIN | 3,895 |
| 49. | MOOSE MOUNTAIN | 3,899 |
| 50. | SNOWY MOUNTAIN | 3,899 |
| 51. | KILBURN MOUNTAIN | 3,892 |
| 52. | SAWTOOTH MOUNTAIN #1 | 3,877 |
| 53. | PANTHER MOUNTAIN | 3,865 |
| 54. | McKENZIE MOUNTAIN | 3,861 |
| 55. | BLUE RIDGE | 3,860 |
| 56. | RIST MOUNTAIN | 3,860 |
| 57. | SENTINEL MOUNTAIN | 3,838 |
| 58. | LYON MOUNTAIN | 3,830 |
| *59. | COUCHSACHRAGA PEAK | 3,820 |
| 60. | SAWTOOTH MOUNTAIN #2 | 3,820 |

The heights used in the above are from the 1953/54 USGS survey.

All of these mountains are in the High Peaks Region except Blue Ridge, located south of Blue Mountain Lake (USGS *Blue Mountain* quad-1990); Lyon Mountain, located southwest of Chazy Lake (USGS *Lyon Mountain/Moffitsville* quads-1968); Panther Mountain located north-east of Wakely Dam (USGS *Indian Lake* quad-1990) and Snowy Mountain located west of Indian Lake (USGS *Indian Lake* quad-1990).

All have marked trails or herd paths except Blue Ridge, Green Mountain, Kilburn Mountain, Lost Pond Peak, Moose Mountain, Sawtooth Mountains #1 and #2 and Sentinel Mountain.

** In the original surveys MacNaughton Mountain was measured at 3,983 feet.
* In the original surveys these mountains were measured at 4,000 or more feet.
† USGS maps and official guide books of the area show this mountain as an unnamed peak. "Lost Pond Peak," although very appropriate, may be an unofficial name. The peak is referred to as Lost Pond Peak throughout this book.

## *About the Author . . .*

John E. Winkler, whose nickname is "Bushwhack," was born in 1941 and is a native Schenectadian. Since graduation from Linton High School in 1959, he has been employed by Benchemark Printing Inc. During 1967-69 he served in the United States Army in Vietnam and Japan, gaining five promotions in the two-year period. He also was awarded the Purple Heart for a wound received in Vietnam.

Over the years he has managed to utilize his vacation time to travel to all fifty states, eleven of the Canadian provinces and territories, and twelve foreign countries.

A member of the Adirondack Mountain Club (ADK) since 1970, he is also a member of the Appalachian Mountain Club (AMC), Adirondack 46ers, Adirondack Council and the Adirondack Nature Conservancy. He spends most of his weekends hiking in the Adirondacks, but is seldom seen on a trail, for he enjoys bushwhacking and exploring most of all. Another of his hobbies is collecting old license plates. He is a member of the Automobile License Plate Collector's Association (ALPCA) and has plates from all fifty states, twelve Canadian provinces and territories, the Canal Zone and Panama.